WILD *at* HEART

A BAND OF BROTHERS

PARTICIPANT'S GUIDE

JOHN ELDREDGE

THOMAS NELSON
Since 1798

NASHVILLE   DALLAS   MEXICO CITY   RIO DE JANEIRO   BEIJING

Published in Nashville, Tennessee, by Thomas Nelson. Thomas Nelson is a
registered trademark of Thomas Nelson, Inc.

The publisher is grateful to Craig McConnell for his writing skills and
collaboration in developing the content for this book.

Published in association with Yates & Yates, LLP, Attorneys and Counselors,
Orange, California.

Unless otherwise noted, Scripture quotations are from the HOLY BIBLE:
NEW INTERNATIONAL VERSION®. Copyright © 1973, 1978, 1984 by
International Bible Society. Used by permission of Zondervan Publishing
House. All rights reserved.

Scripture quotations marked NASB are from the NEW AMERICAN
STANDARD BIBLE®, © Copyright The Lockman Foundation 1960, 1962,
1963, 1968, 1971, 1972, 1973, 1975, 1977. Used by permission.

Scripture quotations marked MSG are from The Message by Eugene H.
Peterson. © 1993, 1994, 1995, 1996, 2000. Used by permission of NavPress
Publishing Group. All rights reserved.

Thomas Nelson, Inc. titles may be purchased in bulk for educational,
business, fund-raising, or sales promotional use. For information, please
e-mail SpecialMarkets@ThomasNelson.com.

ISBN: 978-1-4185-4300-6

Printed in the United States of America
HB 12.27.2019

CONTENTS

CONTENTS

INTRODUCTION

I came so they can have real and eternal life,
more and better life than they ever dreamed of.

—John 10:10 MSG

My gender seems to need little encouragement. It comes naturally, like our innate love of maps. In 1260 Marco Polo headed off to find China, and in 1967, when I was seven, I tried to dig a hole straight through from our backyard with my friend Danny Wilson. We gave up at about eight feet, but it made a great fort. Hannibal crossed his famous Alps, and there comes a day in a boy's life when he first crosses the street and enters the company of the great explorers. Scott and Amundsen raced for the South Pole, Peary and Cook vied for the North, and when last summer I gave my boys some loose change and permission to ride their bikes down to the store to buy a soda, you'd have thought I'd given them a charter to go find the equator. Magellan sailed due west, around the tip of South America—despite warnings that he and his crew would drop off the end of the earth—and Huck Finn headed off down the Mississippi, ignoring similar threats. John Wesley Powell followed the Colorado into the Grand Canyon, even though—no, because—no one had done it before and everyone was saying it couldn't be done . . .

Whatever else those explorers were after, they were also searching for themselves. Deep in a man's heart are some fundamental questions that simply cannot be answered at the kitchen table. Who am I? What am I made of? What am I destined for? It is fear that keeps a man at home where things are neat and orderly and under his control. But the answers to his deepest questions are not to be found on television or in the refrigerator. Out there on the burning desert sands, lost in a trackless waste, Moses received his life's mission and purpose. He was called out, called up into something much bigger than he ever imagined, much more serious than CEO or "prince of Egypt." Under foreign stars, in the dead of night, Jacob received a new name, his real name. No longer was he a shrewd business negotiator, but now he was one who wrestles with God. The wilderness trial of Christ was, at its core, a test of his identity. "If you are who you think you are . . ." If a man is ever to find out who he is and what he's here for, he has got to take that journey for himself.

He has got to get his heart back.[1]

A life few men know and every man yearns for is available! It's a life in which your masculine heart is central, a life so rich and free, so dangerous and yet so exhilarating in its impact, that if you knew now what you could have, you would sell everything to find it. But you know all of this from the echoes in your heart, the hints in your deepest desires, the Voice that has been calling you for a long time, and that's why you're holding this Participant's Guide and viewing this DVD series.

HOW THIS STUDY WORKS

Through this eight-session DVD series, *Wild at Heart*, you'll encounter God in a life-changing way. The design of the Participant's Guide is to facilitate conversation between a small group of men and to provide some direction and questions for going deeper on each topic as an individual between your meeting times.

Before you start, consider the following:

• Start by surrendering yourself to God and his purposes for you in this journey. Yield your mind, volition, heart, spirit, soul, and masculinity to God, and simply invite him to do whatever he'd like.

- Commit yourself to the pace God would have you go through the material. Determine to be responsive to his prodding— maybe take a little more time on a particular section or question, or take a walk or break and allow him to speak to you in a more natural context. A simple way of putting all this is, *walk with God.*

- It would be cruel to your heart to skip the times of reading, reflection, and prayer that will make the dreams that motivated you to participate in this study a reality. Don't fall into a "just get through the material" stride that ends up limiting God and profiting your heart little.

- This series is presented in eight DVD sessions, each about 35 minutes in length. Each session corresponds with topics and material found in the book *Wild at Heart.* The series is designed to be used one session at a time, with small groups of men meeting together for an hour and a half each week to view the DVD and discuss the topic. (By the end of the eight weeks most groups will want to continue with other resources we have available.)

- Each week you should gather at a set time to watch the DVD session together (35 minutes). Read through the "Key Thoughts" (5 minutes) and discuss the group questions, which focus on the DVD material (50 minutes). End your time with prayer. (The "Going Deeper" section is designed for personal reflection.)

- Each member of the group should commit to coming to the weekly gatherings prepared for discussion—have an open spirit, a vulnerable heart, and a thoughtful mind. To foster a spirit of intimacy in your group, limit your group size to no more than eight people.

So, welcome to the journey. It's going to require honesty and a willingness to look at your life from a new perspective. But as you invite God in, you'll find the adventure exciting, the battle challenging, and the beauty of Christ breathtaking. Each week, before you start your study, spend some time in prayer with him, listening to his voice guide you along the way.

PRAYER

Christ, I come thirsty and hungry for more of you. I yield myself completely and totally to you. I give you my expectations for this study. I surrender my heart, mind, spirit, and soul to you, inviting you to touch, deliver, speak, heal, counsel, teach, and train me in whatever areas and ways you choose.

Protect me from the ploys of the evil one. I stand in your authority against all distraction, impatience, diminishment, self-contempt, against every lie, deception, and temptation to turn to any other god for comfort. Fill me with your life that I might more fully live in your Larger Story and with you rescue the hearts and souls of many. Amen.

THE HEART OF A MAN

Then God said, "Let us make man in our image, in our likeness, and let them rule over the fish of the sea and the birds of the air, over the livestock, over all the earth, and over all the creatures that move along the ground." So God created man in his own image, in the image of God he created him; male and female he created them.

—Genesis 1:26–27

Most of us know the oil level of our cars or the state of our investments better than we do the vitality or desires of our heart. And it's completely understandable; there are many things set against you, many distractions and demands upon your life. But these distractions come at a cost: as we tend to our daily demands, we ignore our masculine heart.

In the first session of our series, Bart, Morgan, Craig, and Gary joined me for a day of horseback riding up in the Colorado Rockies and talking about the heart of a man.

WATCH PART 1:
THE HEART OF A MAN

KEY THOUGHTS

This session corresponds with chapters 1 and 2 from *Wild at Heart*. The major points of these chapters are summarized here.

———— ⨀ ————

- God made the masculine heart and sets it within every man he creates.

- There is, therefore, something deep and true and universal to the masculine heart. And it's been lost—or better, driven into hiding.

- You cannot get your masculine heart back through duty and obligation. You must pursue it with your deepest desires. What makes you come alive?

- Somewhere down in your heart are three core desires: a battle to fight, an adventure to live, and a beauty to rescue.

- God, too, has each of these longings lodged deep in his heart: the yearning for a battle to fight is deep in the heart of God. He, too, longs for adventure and risk—far more than we do. And he has a beauty to rescue, whom he pursues with amazing passion.

DISCUSS

After watching the DVD segment, it should be clear that the men in this group have varying levels of comfort when it comes to riding horses. Some of us had a lot of experience on horseback. A few of us were very anxious about the day.

❖ With whom did you identify most when it comes to riding horses? Why?

❖ As you listened in on the conversation these men were having about the true nature of the masculine heart, what struck you as the most important, the most relevant point they made?

God made the masculine heart, set it within
every man, and thereby offers him an *invitation*:
Come, and live out what I meant you to be.[1]

❖ The major theme of this book is the core desires of a man's soul—a battle to fight, an adventure to live, a beauty to rescue. Can you identify these in your life? Where or how?

Craig talked about his boyhood neighborhood and how he and his friends loved to play army. His little platoon defended the neighborhood with popguns and tangerine grenades.

❖ What adventures or games did you play and love when you were a boy?

In the same way God called Jesus into the wilderness to be tempted and took Elijah into the wilderness to find his true destiny, he calls a man out of his comfort zone to discover who he is. It is in the wilderness that God shows us we have what it takes to live the very life for which God created us. Unless we step out into that adventure God has for us, we will never learn it anywhere else. It cannot be learned on the sofa.

❖ What comfort zone is God calling you out of?

❖ What adventure is he leading you into?

❖ Is it a tame, controllable adventure or a wild and unpredictable one?

❖ Walter Bruggerman describes God as "wild, unfettered, dangerous, and free." Is that how you would describe the God you've been told about?

You remember that wild man Samson? He's got a pretty impressive masculine résumé: killed a lion with his bare hands, pummeled and stripped thirty Philistines when they used his wife against him, and finally, after they burned her to death, he killed a thousand men with the jawbone of a donkey. Not a guy to mess with. But did you notice? All those events happened when *"the Spirit of the LORD came upon him"* (Judges 15:14, emphasis added). Now, let me make one thing clear: I am not advocating a sort of "macho man" image. I'm not suggesting we all head off to the gym and then to the beach to kick sand in the faces of wimpy Pharisees. I am attempting to rescue us from a very, very mistaken image we have of God—especially of Jesus—and therefore of men as his image-bearers. Dorothy Sayers wrote that the church has "very efficiently pared the claws of the Lion of Judah," making him "a fitting household pet for pale curates and pious old ladies." Is that the God you find in the Bible?[2]

"Desire" is central in mapping out your masculine journey. Don't ask what the world needs; ask what makes you come alive: that's what the world needs!

❖ Consider what makes you come alive. With that in mind, finish this sentence: "For the rest of my life, I want to _____."

❖ What, beginning this week, would that look like?

PRAYER

Turn to the Lord in prayer, giving him the desires that have lain in your heart for years or asking him to reveal the desires that you can't seem to put your finger on. Trust him to show you the way to start your journey.

O Lord, open wide the eyes of my soul that I might see the true yearnings of my heart. Uncover my desire for adventure, battle, and beauty. Begin to dismantle all the messages that have challenged and assaulted your design of me. May your invitation to life as a man be forever before me. I accept the invitation to live from my deep heart. Father, use the words of this book and the meditations of my heart to guide, shape, and direct me in this journey that I might be the man you designed me to be. I ask this in the name of Jesus. Amen.

Listen to me, you who pursue righteousness
and who seek the LORD:
Look to the rock from which you were cut
and to the quarry from which you were hewn.

—Isaiah 51:1

GOING DEEPER

If you truly want to embrace the untamed journey Christ has planned for you, you won't be satisfied thinking about this just once a week. This section is designed for you to study the topic further on your own after your group meets. So make some time throughout the week (on your lunch break, instead of watching TV at night, or in the early morning) to read through these questions and consider what God is saying to you here.

It can be very awkward for men to share their hearts. It's slow going and uncomfortable—territory we're not used to traversing. But the alternatives are to hide in isolation or live as an impostor, and who wants that?

❖ How did the group conversation and interaction go when you met? Did you find yourself reluctant to share your thoughts? Did you temper them, or do you regret saying too much?

❖ What did God say to you as you were meeting with the men? Did he impress anything on you during that time?

❖ What do you hope to achieve in this group? Do you have a goal in mind? Are you willing to let God change that goal, if that is his will?

The masculine heart needs a place where nothing is pre-fabricated, modular, nonfat, zip-locked, franchised, on-line, and microwavable. Where there are no deadlines, cell phones, or committee meetings. Where there is room for the soul. Where, finally, the geography around us corresponds to the geography of our heart.[3]

There is the life we were *meant for* and the men we were *created to be* . . . and then there is the life we *have* and the men we *find ourselves* to be. They are often worlds apart.

❖ How is the man you find yourself to be different from the man you were created to be?

❖ At this stage of your life, what is your great battle? Is it on the surface (making more money, getting the kids to behave, reducing the hassles of life?), or is it deeper? Are you willing to share it with the men in your group?

❖ Where is your great adventure? What real risk have you been swept up into? (Is anything in your life more compelling than watching sports, following stocks, or viewing the adventures of others on TV?)

❖ And who is the beauty you are fighting for? (Is there a woman in your life who stirs you to leap through a ring of fire to win her?)

Dr. Tremper Longman III, the coauthor of *Bold Love*, wrote, "Virtually every book of the Bible—Old and New Testaments—and almost every page tells us about God's warring activity."

❖ Have you ever considered the Bible to be an account of a great battle that God himself is fighting?

❖ How does this help you interpret all that's going on around you in your life today?

PRAYER

Go back to God and talk with him about where your heart is on all you've discussed and thought about this week. End your time here praying, in your own words, the prayer on page 15.

NEXT WEEK

Next week your group will discuss the second DVD segment, "The Poser and the Question." In order to be prepared to share your thoughts with your group, read chapter 3 from *Wild at Heart* this week prior to your group meeting.

PART 1

NOTES

PART

2

THE POSER AND THE QUESTION

I was afraid because I was naked; so I hid.

—Genesis 3:10

What kind of life would you have to live to eliminate all fear or risk? No matter how many insurance policies you purchase, helmets you wear, personas you create, or doors you lock, one of the certain lessons life teaches us is that there is no escaping fear and risk.

In this DVD we'll be talking about our deepest fear while rapelling a one-hundred-foot cliff. But our fear isn't heights; the central fear all men share is that we will be exposed as an impostor, a poser, a man who doesn't really have what it takes.

WATCH PART 2:
THE POSER AND THE QUESTION

KEY THOUGHTS

This session corresponds with chapter 3 from *Wild at Heart*. The major points of this chapter are summarized here.

⁓⁓⁓

- The world is filled with caricatures of masculinity—posers—but very few real men.

- And every one of us posers shares a deepest fear: to be found out, exposed as an impostor.

- The reason, in part, goes back to Adam's fall—and the way every man since him has also fallen to the temptations of sin.

- Men handle their fallen nature by either becoming violent (driven) or retreating (passive)—we mishandle our strength.

DISCUSS

Each of us had our turn rappelling. Even a couple of the experienced guys admitted that anytime you step backward off a one-hundred-foot cliff, you feel a bit of the "pucker" factor.

❖ How would you do rappelling?

A man is fierce . . . passionate . . . wild at heart? You wouldn't know it from what normally walks around in a pair of trousers. If that's true, how come there are so many lonely women, so many fatherless children, so few *men* around? Why is it that the world seems filled with "caricatures" of masculinity? How come when men look in their hearts they don't discover something valiant and dangerous, but instead find anger, lust, and fear? Why is that?[1]

In last week's "Going Deeper" section, you were asked a question about vulnerability. The success of this group is based proportionately on the willingness of everyone to be honest and open with one another.

❖ Do you feel you were an open book last week?

❖ Did you write down a goal you have for this group? If so, what is it?

We are made in the image of the Lion of Judah to fight great battles, take great adventures, and rescue the beauty. When I asked the guys if that's how they feel inside most of the time, Gary admitted that in a variety of circumstances, what he felt most was fear. It's the fear that comes from not knowing what to do and being afraid to ask.

❖ Describe how you feel inside most days. (Strong, unfettered, free, alive, adventurous, fearful, apprehensive, hesitant?)

When the woman saw that the fruit of the tree was good for food and pleasing to the eye, and also desirable for gaining wisdom, she took some and ate it. She also gave some to her husband, who was with her, and he ate it. Then the eyes of both of them were opened, and they realized they were naked; so they sewed fig leaves together and made coverings for themselves. Then the man and his wife heard the sound of the LORD God as he was walking in the garden in the cool of the day, and they hid from the LORD God among the trees of the garden. But the LORD God called to the man, "Where are you?" He answered, "I heard you in the garden, and I was afraid because I was naked; so I hid."

—Genesis 3:6–10

❖ How do you feel about the fact that Adam was standing right there when Eve was being tempted, and he didn't do a thing?

❖ Can you see that same passivity in your own life?

Men are geniuses at designing elaborate fig leaves, brilliant disguises that we call "personality." Like Adam, we are afraid we aren't what we should be. So we create "The Poser" to hide behind. When we ask ourselves, "Have I got what it takes?" we fear we don't, and the poser is born. But this disguise has become so second nature to us that most men are only half-aware of the ways they hide.

❖ How are you hiding these days? How do you pose?

❖ Has it worked/ been effective?

God comes to all of us as he came to Adam—calling to us, asking us to come out of hiding, to face our fears, to walk with him into our true strength. It's in the intentional movement away from hiding and into honesty that we discover our true selves. But to move away from the safety of our effective hiding feels about the same as jumping off a cliff: counterintuitive, unnatural, wrong!

❖ What is the cliff God would have you "jump off" as a man? (If your reaction to jumping off this cliff is "Oh, my God, help me," it's a real cliff. Anything else is posing.)

❖ What's the first step you will take to come out of hiding and reveal your true self to the others you're "doing life" with?

PRAYER

It's scary, but we have to go there. Only when we leave the poser behind will we begin to live as men, and in doing so find real strength, adventure, and beauty. Ask God to give you the courage to take those first steps today, even within the next hour.

Search me, O God, and know my heart. Try me and know my fearful thoughts. Reveal to me the ways I pose and hide, and O God, lead me in the everlasting way, the way of truth and strength. May I live with passion and zeal; may my soul be captured by you for something big, noble, and worthy of your kingdom. Remove the quiet desperation of my soul. Chase away resignation, anger, and the addictions I run to. Free me to be a strong, passionate, and dangerous man . . . as you created me to be. Draw me beyond the battles I know I can win; lure me to larger adventures . . . speak with power those words I long to hear: "You have what it takes." I ask all this in Jesus' name. Amen.

Surely you desire truth in the inner parts.

—Psalm 51:6

GOING DEEPER

Read through chapter 3 from *Wild at Heart* again, and answer these questions on your own during a lunch break, over a cup of coffee in the morning, or at the end of the day.

———❦———

❖ This was your second meeting—how did the group conversation and interaction go today? Did you feel an internal (or external) pressure to pose or to hide during the discussion time?

❖ What did God say to you as you were meeting with the men?

As you enter into what may be your first really candid picture of yourself as a man, consider two things. First, this isn't the end of the story. We're only in the second session, and if there weren't hope for us posers, I wouldn't have written this book. Second, this isn't going to be helpful if you try to sound like a better guy than you really are; nor is it helpful to assume a false Christian humility because that's the "spiritual" thing to do. As David says in Psalm 51, God desires truth in our inmost being. Be honest—no more, no less.

Something's gone wrong in men, and we know it. Something about us, or in us, is just not what we know it was meant to be. What's *happened* to us? Why aren't we more fierce, daring, and passionate? You're going to need to be really honest— brutally honest—if you hope to continue the journey from here. Remember, we have to cross the desert, the no-man's-land, before winning the promised land.[2]

❖ What is your definition of "a man"?

❖ How do you measure up to that definition? (Write a simple, candid description of yourself as a man. You don't need to show this to anyone.)

Men are expected to be good at almost everything—to come through for ourselves and others in a pinch. Life can't throw anything at us we can't handle, or can it? The truth is, each of us fears the moment we won't be able to handle the load we've been given. When the going gets rough, when it really matters, can we really pull it off?

❖ In what area of your life do you fear you'll break down or be exposed as a fake? (For example, do you fear you'll crack under the pressure at work? Do you dread expressing emotion to your family? Do you fake a "masculine" confidence on topics like finance, sports, or machinery when you're with the guys?)

❖ Where are you avoiding exposure?

❖ So, how do you want to live differently?

❖ What will have to change for you to live differently? (The answer to this question may be something like a new mind-set, a little more vulnerability with your wife or friends, a job change and relocation. If the changes you make will affect other people, give careful consideration here to the ways they need to be involved.)

PRAYER

You've been asked to consider making some major changes to your life. That's certainly not something to do alone. End your time here praying. In your own words, pray the prayer given on page 29.

NEXT WEEK

Next week your group will discuss the third DVD segment, "The Wound." In order to be prepared to share your thoughts with your group, read chapters 4 and 5 from *Wild at Heart* this week prior to your group meeting.

PART

3

THE WOUND

Deal well with me for your name's sake;
out of the goodness of your love, deliver me.
For I am poor and needy, and my heart is wounded within me.

—Psalm 109:21–22

Every man carries a wound. I have never met a man without one. No matter how good your life may have seemed to you, you live in a broken world full of broken people. Your mother and father, no matter how wonderful, couldn't have been perfect. She is a daughter of Eve, and he a son of Adam. So there is no crossing through this country without taking a wound. And every wound, whether it's assaultive or passive, delivers with it a message. The message feels final and true, absolutely true, because it is delivered with such force. Our reaction to it shapes our personality in very significant ways. From that flows the false self. Most of the men you meet are living out a false self, a pose, which is directly related to each one's wound.

WATCH PART 3:
THE WOUND

KEY THOUGHTS

This session corresponds with chapters 4 and 5 from *Wild at Heart*. The major points of this chapter are summarized here:

- Every boy has two questions in life: Do I have what it takes? Am I powerful?

- Most men live their lives either haunted by the Question or crippled by the answer they've been given.

- Masculinity is *bestowed*. A boy learns who he is and what he's got from a man, or the company of men.

- Yet every boy, in his journey to become a man, takes an arrow in the center of his heart, in the place of his strength. And the wound is nearly always given by his father.

- With the wound comes a message, and out of the message we make a vow to do what it takes to make sure we're not wounded that way again.

- The result is a false self—a deep uncertainty in the soul, and a driven or passive man on the outside.

DISCUSS

❖ Every little boy looks up to his father as a hero, a role model—at least for a little while. What was your relationship with your dad like when you were a young child? Share the memory of a happy childhood moment with your father.

In the video and the chapters we've read, we've seen that most of us carry a wound that was bestowed upon us by our fathers, whether intentionally or accidentally. Even if your father was a good man, he wasn't Jesus Christ, so at some point he likely wounded you. Share with the group part of your story:

❖ What things did you do together with your dad when you were a child?

❖ What was your dad's message to you in answer to your Question, "Do I have what it takes?" What did your dad teach you about yourself as a man?

❖ Describe the moment in which you decided whether or not you were powerful (the second question all boys share). What were the circumstances? Who witnessed the event, if there was one? What did you do with the knowledge?

❖ Now, share your wound. (If tears come . . . that's okay. The tears are good, the grief necessary. This is part of the journey, not all of the journey).

We are wounded, and with that wound comes a message—a lie about us and about the world and often about God too. The wound and lie then lead to a vow, a resolution to never, ever do again whatever it was that might have brought the wound. From that vow we develop a false self.

❖ What was your wound's message?

❖ What is the vow you made in response to your message?

❖ How have the message and the vow shaped your life? Can you see any tangible effects of the message in your relationships, habits, or daily living?

Men either overcompensate for their wound and become determined to prove the message wrong, or they shrink back, attempting to avoid the "certainty" of the wound's message. Often it's an odd mixture of both.

❖ Which has been your story?

As we move forward in our masculine journey, God steps into our fathers' place and fathers us, inviting us back into those areas of fear and woundedness so that he can walk with us, coming by our side to offer us validation and healing.

❖ Why would God want to raise our awareness of our wound?

PRAYER

God has a reason for asking you to consider your wound, despite the pain it may cause you. Trust him with it, and believe that, in his hands, your wound can become your freedom.

———⚬⚬⚬———

O God, it's true. My heart is wounded within me. Come to me, dear Jesus, speak to my heart such a strong and sure word; affirm my masculinity, and grant me the ears to hear you speak those life-giving words. Take me now on the journey of my heart's recovery. Show me more clearly the assault I've endured, and what I've done with my heart over these years. Only keep my heart, I pray, and be my guide at every step. In your name I pray. Amen.

> Weeping may last for the night,
> But a shout of joy comes in the morning.
>
> **—Psalm 30:5** NASB

GOING DEEPER

This clearly is one of the more difficult and painful sessions. It would be easy yet tragic to quickly move on to the next topic. Instead, read through chapters 4 and 5 from *Wild at Heart* again, and set aside some private time to answer these questions on your own this week.

❖ How did the group conversation and interaction go today? Did you find yourself reluctant to share your story? Why or why not?

❖ What did God say to you as you were meeting with the men?

To clarify two things when it comes to finding our "wound": First, it is not necessarily one clear wound, given on an unforgettable day you remember in detail. Many men can recall the day they received a soul wound from their father that somehow defined the rest of their relationship with him. But for others, it is an accumulation of subtle wounds and messages, given over time. Second, I believe that every man carries a wound. No matter how good a man your father was, and may still be, he is not Jesus Christ. Every father is a son of Adam, and every father himself grew up in a world far from Eden. Given these two biblical truths, be very, very cautious to come to the conclusion that you somehow escaped the father-wound. Your father may have repented deeply of his own false self as a young man, and been substantially healed of his own wound before he fathered you. But that is a rare, rare case.[1]

❖ Describe a time in your life when you heard words like those Jesus heard from his Father—"I am deeply proud of you; you have what it takes."

❖ What do those memories or the lack of them stir up in you?

❖ Was it hard to identify your wound? If so, why do you suppose? If not, why so?

The passive wounds are not as obvious. Passive fathers give a blow that is harder to define, because it didn't come as a blow; it came as an absence. Words unspoken, affection withheld . . . As Bly says, "Not receiving any blessing from your father is an injury . . . Not seeing your father when you are small, never being with him, having a remote father, an absent father, a workaholic father, is an injury." . . . In the case of violent fathers, the boy's Question is answered in a devastating way. "Do I have what it takes? Am I a man, Papa?" No, you are a mama's boy, an idiot, a faggot, a seagull. Those are defining sentences that shape a man's life. The assault wounds are like a shotgun blast to the chest. This can get unspeakably evil when it involves physical, sexual, or verbal abuse carried on for years. Violent fathers give a wound that is easier to recognize.[2]

* In the DVD segment you watched with the group, Craig shared that his father was violent, while mine was more passive in wounding me. Which was yours?

* How has your wound's message affected you emotionally?

* Are you willing to believe that the message may be a lie? What will it take for you to reject that message?

❖ What *would* you have loved to hear from your father? (If your father bestowed a clear sense of masculinity upon you, give great thanks to God for having blessed you with a father who gave to you what so few have had. Ask God to carry you on in your masculine journey, to take you deeper and farther into your heart.)

PRAYER

You've opened some wounds from your past—for some men these are deep, painful gashes that have not lost their sting as time has passed. Take this hurt to God, and ask him to set you on the road to healing. End your time here praying, in your own words, the prayer given on page 40.

NEXT WEEK

Next week your group will discuss the fourth DVD segment, "Healing the Wound." In order to be prepared to share your thoughts with your group, read chapters 6 and 7 from *Wild at Heart* this week.

PART

4

HEALING THE WOUND

The Spirit of the Lord is on me,
because he has anointed me
to preach good news to the poor.
He has sent me to proclaim freedom for the prisoners
and recovery of sight for the blind,
to release the oppressed,
to proclaim the year of the Lord's favor.

—Luke 4:18–19

Frederick Buechner was so right when he said that we bury our wound deep, and after a while we never take it out again, let alone speak of it. But take it out we must—or even better, enter into it. Christ must *touch* us, and touch us *where we hurt most.*

The biggest adventure so far in this series is this one . . . time alone with God, being with the God who longs to touch us, to heal us. It doesn't come easy, but adventure never does. This week we'll take our wound and its message to God to listen to all he has to say to us. What we're seeking is a deeper healing of our wound(s), and that can only come from God.

WATCH PART 4:
HEALING THE WOUND

KEY THOUGHTS

This session corresponds with chapters 6 and 7 from *Wild at Heart*. The major points of this chapter are summarized here.

——⁂——

- It's not a sign of weakness that you need God desperately—you were meant to live in a deeply dependent relationship with him.

- The healing of your wound begins by no longer despising those broken places within you—after all, your wound was not your fault.

- You'll find the healing of your masculine soul through a process that, by its nature, has to be very personal.

- God has a new name for you, and hearing that name is a deep part of the healing process. That name reveals your true strength, your glory, and your calling.

DISCUSS

❖ Boys are notorious for getting into mischief growing up. Often, this comes with broken bones and trips to the ER. What's the most painful injury you've experienced? Or, if you haven't broken a bone, or hurt yourself physically in any other serious way, what reckless things did you do as a kid that should have gotten you hurt?

❖ What in this DVD session struck you as the most important, the most relevant point?

The "Good News" of Christianity, at its core, isn't about us being more obedient dutiful men; rather, it's the offer of Christ to heal our broken hearts and restore and set us free. That was Christ's mission in his own words (read Luke 4:18).

❖ React to the idea that, of all the things Christ came to do, healing your broken heart is at the top of his list.

❖ Does this surprise you? Do you doubt it? Why or why not?

"Men are taught over and over when they are boys that a wound that hurts is shameful," notes Bly. "A wound that stops you from continuing to play is a girlish wound. He who is truly a man keeps walking, dragging his guts behind." Like a man who's broken his leg in a marathon, he finishes the race even if he has to crawl and he doesn't say a word about it. That sort of misunderstanding is why for most of us, our wound is an immense source of shame. A man's not supposed to get hurt; he's certainly not supposed to let it really matter. We've seen too many movies where the good guy takes an arrow, just breaks it off, and keeps on fighting; or maybe he gets shot but is still able to leap across a canyon and get the bad guys. And so most men minimize their wound.[1]

❖ Consider the ways you were taught or shown, as a boy, to "walk it off" when you were wounded—physically or emotionally. How have you mishandled your wound?

Most men *minimize* their wound. They either deny it outright ("I had a pretty good life"), leave it in the past ("That was a long time ago, and I've gotten over it"), or minimize the impact of the wound ("Lots of tough things happen to people . . . So?"). Other men may admit the wound but mishandle it because they *embrace* it or its message. This is seen when men believe they deserved any wrongs done to them as a child, or when they take on a victim mentality and let the wound define them ("I'm weak . . . take care of me. And don't ever require me to be a man").

❖ Which of these describes what you've done with your wound and how you have handled it?

A man's core Question does not go away. He may
try for years to shove it out of his awareness, and just
"get on with life." But it does not go away. It is a hun-
ger so essential to our soul that it will compel us to find
a resolution. In truth, it drives everything we do.[2]

❖ Where are you going for the masculine validation you need? To what or whom are you looking?

❖ As you think about the components of a way to healing, which of these strike you as something you have done? Want to do? Or don't really understand?

- Surrendering yourself and your wounds to God

- Renouncing the vow, those efforts you've made to live without God

- Giving God permission to meet you in your wounds and restore you as he promised (Isaiah 61)

- Asking God what he thinks of you—do you have what it takes?—and staying with the question until you hear him

God will come and will heal. But we need to let him. The hardest part about hearing God validate us, hearing his new name for us, is letting it be true. In our time alone with God on the DVD, I heard, "You are the real deal." Craig heard, "You do have something to offer—you are a warrior shepherd for my kingdom." Bart heard, "You have a strength that's yet to be revealed."

❖ Go ahead—embarrass yourself. What would you really love for God to say to you?

The masculine journey comes alive and we take our biggest step into the frontier when we ask God to father us. God wants to tell us our true names, tell us what we need to hear. But he also wants to take us through a series of initiations where we can discover who we really are as men, and that we do have what it takes.

❖ How might God be doing that now, in this season of your life?

PRAYER

How can we hear what God wants to tell us if we don't come to him to listen? Pray the prayer below, but then spend some time in silence before God, listening to what he wants to tell you. What he says just may change your life.

Father, who am I to you? You are my true Father—my Creator, my Redeemer, and my Sustainer. You know the man you had in mind when you made me. You know my true name. O Father, I ask you to speak to me, to reveal to me my true strength and my real name. Open my eyes that I might see; give me ears to hear your voice. Father, I ask that you speak it not once, but again and again so that I might really receive it. And grant me the courage to receive what you say and the faith to believe it. Thank you for this great work you have begun in my heart. Take me deeper, Lord— deeper into healing, deeper into strength, deeper into my true name. Seal this work in my heart with your blood, and let not one ounce be stolen from me. Carry me on, I pray in your name. Amen.

Praise the LORD.
How good it is to sing praises to our God,
how pleasant and fitting to praise him! . . .
He heals the brokenhearted
and binds up their wounds.

—Psalm 147:1, 3

GOING DEEPER

Read through chapters 6 and 7 from *Wild at Heart* again, and answer these questions on your own this week.

―――∽∾∾―――

❖ First, how did the group conversation and interaction go this week?

❖ What would you love God to say to you about yourself, as a man?

The way in which God heals your wound is a deeply personal process. For one man it happens in a dramatic moment; for another, it takes place over time. Even after we've experienced some real healing, God will often take us back again, a year or two later, for a deeper work of healing. There is a way toward healing—a process that has helped me and many other men. Think about each component of this journey and pray the simple prayer following it.

Surrender

Dear Jesus, I am yours. You have ransomed me with your own life, bought me with your own blood. Forgive me for all my years of independence—all my striving, all my retreating, all my self-centeredness and self-determination. I give myself back to you—all of me. I give my body to you as a living sacrifice. I give my soul to you as well—my desperate search for life and love and validation, all my self-protecting, all those parts in me I like and all those I do not like. I give to you my spirit also, to be restored in union with you, for as the Scripture says, "He who unites himself with the Lord is one with him in spirit."[3] Forgive me, cleanse me, take me and make me utterly yours. In your name I pray. Amen.

Renounce the Vow

Jesus, I renounce every vow I've made to seal off my wound and protect myself from further pain. Reveal to me what those vows were. [If you can name them specifically, do so, and renounce them.] *I break every agreement I have made with the lies that came with my wounds, the lies of Satan, and I make all agreement with you, Jesus. I give the protection of my heart and soul back to you; I trust you with all that is within me. In your name I pray. Amen.*

Invitation

And precious Jesus, I invite you into the wounded places of my heart, give you permission to enter every broken place, every young and orphaned part of me. Come, dear Lord, and meet me there. Bind up my heart as you promised to do; heal me and make my heart whole and healthy. Release my heart from every form of captivity and from every form of bondage. Restore and set free my heart, my soul, my mind, and my strength. Help me to mourn, and comfort me as I do. Grant my soul that noble crown of strength instead of ashes; anoint me with the oil of gladness in every grieving part; grant me a garment of praise in place of a spirit of despair. O come to me, Jesus, and surround me with your healing presence. Restore me through union with you. I ask in your name. Amen.

Grieve

Yes, Jesus—I confess that it mattered. It mattered deeply. Come into my soul and release the grief and tears bottled up within me. Help me to grieve my own wounds and sorrows. Amen.

God's Love

Father, strengthen me with your true strength, by your Spirit in my innermost being, so that Jesus may live intimately in my heart. O let me be rooted and grounded in love, so that I, too, with all your precious saints, may know the fullness of the love of Jesus for me—its height and depth, its length and breadth. Let me be filled with real knowledge of your love—even though I will never fully reason it or comprehend it—so that I might be filled with all the life and power you have for me. Do this in me, beyond all that I am able to ask or imagine. Amen.

Forgiveness

Jesus, I choose to forgive my father for all the pain and all the wounds he gave to me. [It will help to be very specific here—to name those wounds and events.] It was wrong, it hurt me deeply, and I choose now to pardon him, because your sacrifice on the cross was enough to pay for these sins. I release my father to you. I also release any bitterness I've harbored toward him, and I ask you to come and cleanse these wounds and heal them. In your name I pray. Amen.

Christ will do what he came to do . . . The deep prayers of your heart have been heard and answered. God is good.

PRAYER

I must alert you to the reality that the battle may get intense for you. The enemy, the accuser, is not going to take this one lying down. The last thing he wants is your healing and the restoration of your masculine heart and strength. Spend time in prayer, rejecting all accusation and fighting off all discouragement and resignation. God may speak something immediately to you, and then confirm it over time, or he may unfold this to you over the next few months. Don't be discouraged and don't give up. Hang in there—this is part of your warrior training.

NEXT WEEK

Next week your group will discuss the fifth DVD segment, "A Battle to Fight." In order to be prepared to share your thoughts with your group, read chapters 8 and 9 from *Wild at Heart* this week prior to your group meeting.

NOTES

PART

5

A BATTLE TO FIGHT

The LORD is a warrior, the LORD is his name.

—Exodus 15:3

God, who is a great warrior, created man in his image. God set within us a warrior heart because he has created us to join him in his war against evil, and if we're going to find our part in God's story, if we're going to be the men that he made us to be, we have to get that part of our heart back.

Over the next three sessions, we are shifting from the healing of your masculine heart to the *release* of your heart into the battle, the adventure, and the beauty. We're going to start with the battle because (1) it's where most men get taken out, and, (2) if you want the adventure and the beauty, you're going to have to fight for them!

WATCH PART 5:
A BATTLE TO FIGHT

KEY THOUGHTS

This session corresponds with chapters 8 and 9 from *Wild at Heart*. The major points of this chapter are summarized here:

———— ✸✸✸ ————

- A man must have a battle to fight, a great mission for his life that involves but also transcends home and family.

- To beat the enemy called the flesh, you must embrace the promise of the new covenant—that God has given you a new heart.

- To beat the enemy of the world, you must expose the counterfeits it offers you—counterfeit battles, adventures, and beauties.

- And as for Satan . . . you begin by bringing him back into the context of your real beliefs and the way you evaluate life.

- Stage One of Satan's strategy is always: "I'm not here—this is just you." Most men live their whole lives duped at that level.

- In Stage Two Satan moves to intimidation—trying to threaten us back in line.

- At Stage Three he offers us a deal of some kind.

- We've been given our aggressive heart to fight aggressively. And God has provided the weapons we need.

DISCUSS

❖ Have you ever been in a fistfight? What was the issue you were defending? Why did you feel so strongly about it?

From cover to cover the whole Bible is a story of war. In the DVD, we shared some of our recollections of Scripture that spoke of God being a warrior: the Exodus, Jericho, Gideon, King David, Nehemiah, and the Prophets. (We actually could have gone on and on.) Scripture is clear that, among the many names and descriptions attributed to God, his role as warrior is a predominate one (see Exodus 15:3, for example).

❖ Do you picture God as a warring God? How does this make you feel?

❖ What has been the mental picture of Christ you've had? Can you imagine him as a warrior?

As I said in the video, God sets within each of us a warrior heart. If we're going to be the men he made us to be, we've got to get that part of our hearts back. We have to start with the battle to recover the warrior heart, the warrior image of God in us, because if we can get that back, then we're equipped to live the adventure God has for us and to rescue the beauty. The first battle is to get our heart back and recover the warrior within.

We could probably divide all the guys in the world into three categories:

- Guys who have no battle
- Guys who have the wrong kind of battle (e.g., King Saul trying to kill David)
- Guys who know their true place in the battle

❖ Which category do you see yourself being in currently? Explain why.

❖ If you feel you know your true place in the battle, what is it?

❖ A man needs a battle to fight. Without a great battle, a great cause to give ourselves to, we battle for the smallest things. Life requires a man to be fierce . . . is that true of most men you know?

❖ What would you say is the biggest battle you're fighting right now in your life?

We live in a world where spiritual powers are at war. The day is coming when the lion lies down with the lamb, but that's not now; that's later . . . now it's battle. And any one of us who claims to be a Christian is playing a role in this battle, whether you like it or not. This isn't a fairy tale; it's real. We must begin to see life as an assault against our hearts and against the image of God in us. We must begin to resist, to fight back.

❖ How have you understood that you are living in a world at war?

❖ Has spiritual warfare been a serious part of your Christian life? Why or why not?

❖ Which of Satan's strategies has been at play in your life? Explain.

❖ What will you do to fight back?

PRAYER

We are mere men, called into battle against the powers of evil in this world. It is a fight we cannot do alone—we require God's strength to survive. Pray, asking him to give you his strength and his will to fight.

━━━∽∾∽━━━

Strengthen me with your strength, O God. Rally my soul into this great battle. Dear Jesus, expose the enemies of my heart and my life so that I may see the battle lines more clearly. Show me my place; speak my name to me again. Grant me a vision for my life, and grant me the cunning mind of a warrior. Sustain me in this battle and in this journey, that in your name I might gain the victory. I pray in the mighty power of Jesus' name. Amen.

> Be self-controlled and alert. Your enemy the devil
> prowls around like a roaring lion looking for some-
> one to devour. Resist him, standing firm in the faith,
> because you know that your brothers throughout the
> world are undergoing the same kind of sufferings.
>
> **—1 Peter 5:8–9**

GOING DEEPER

Read through chapters 8 and 9 from *Wild at Heart* again, and answer these questions on your own this week.

❖ What was the discussion and interaction like as a group? Did it go well? Was it rough? disjointed? Can you see ways the enemy has tried to disrupt and destroy your group?

A man must have a battle to fight, a great mission to his life that involves and yet transcends even home and family. He must have a cause to which he is devoted even unto death, for this is written into the fabric of his being. Listen carefully now: *You do.* That is why God created you—to be his intimate *ally*, to join him in the Great Battle. You have a specific place in the line, a mission God made you for. That is why it is so essential to hear from God about your true name, because in that name is the mission of your life. Churchill was called upon to lead the British through the desperate hours of World War II. He said, "I felt as if I were walking with destiny, and that all my past life had been but a preparation for this hour and for this trial." The same is true of you; [*you* are "walking with destiny" and] *your whole* life has been preparation ["for this hour and for this trial."][1]

❖ What, specifically, is your great mission? What great battle is God inviting you into as his ally?

❖ As followers of Christ, there are three enemies we must battle: the flesh, the world, and the devil. Describe how your flesh battles against your true good heart.

❖ How does the world assault your walk with God?

❖ Where in your life do you suspect that the devil is attacking your heart?

❖ Do you feel adequately trained and sufficiently equipped to battle these foes?

❖ Read 1 Peter 5:8–9 and James 4:7. What is God saying through Peter and James that you must do in your battle against the adversary?

❖ We've all made agreements with the enemy's lies and accusations (e.g., *My heart is bad; I'm basically a slob; I'm a lustful man to the core; I'm arrogant and self-centered; I'm a coward*). Can you name yours?

❖ Read Ephesians 6:10–17. What is Paul's simple instruction?

Against the evil one we wear the armor of God. That God has provided weapons of war for us sure makes a lot more sense if our days were like a scene from *Saving Private Ryan*. How many Christians have read over those passages about the shield of faith and the helmet of salvation and have never really known what to do with them? *What lovely poetic imagery; I wonder what it means.* It means that God has given you armor, and you'd better put it on. Every day.

❖ What do you do to put on the armor of God daily?

PRAYER

In order to release ourselves from the enemy's snares, we must renounce any agreements we've made with him that stem from our wounds. Pray this simple prayer against the agreements you've made.

———— ⌘ ————

Dear Jesus, forgive me for making these agreements with the enemy. Forgive me for giving him ground in my life. I break those agreements now. I break all agreements with [get specific here—name them] *and I renounce the lie. I cancel any ground I have given Satan in my life, and I make all agreement with you, Lord Jesus. You are the Way and the Truth and the Life; all the ground that I once gave to Satan I now give to you and you alone. In the authority of your name I pray. Amen.*

NEXT WEEK

Next week your group will discuss the sixth DVD segment, "An Adventure to Live." In order to be prepared to share your thoughts with your group, read chapter 11 from *Wild at Heart* this week prior to your group meeting.

PART

6

AN ADVENTURE TO LIVE

*"Lord, if it's you," Peter replied, "tell me
to come to you on the water."
"Come," he said.
Then Peter got down out of the boat, walked
on the water and came toward Jesus.*

—Matthew 14:28–29

Life is not a problem to be solved; it is an adventure to be lived. That is the nature of it and has been since the beginning, when God set the dangerous stage for this high-stakes drama and called the whole wild enterprise good. He rigged the world in such a way that it only works when we embrace risk as the theme of our lives, which is to say, only when we live by faith. A man just won't be happy until he has adventure in his work, in his love, and in his spiritual life.

WATCH PART 6:
AN ADVENTURE TO LIVE

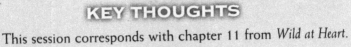

KEY THOUGHTS

This session corresponds with chapter 11 from *Wild at Heart*. The major points of this chapter are summarized here.

⸺⸺

- Life is not a problem to be solved; it is an adventure to be lived.

- A man just won't be happy until he has adventure in his work, his love, and his spiritual life.

- Most men sacrifice their dreams because of fear, and they live out a script someone else wrote for them.

- Your true calling is written on your true heart, and you'll discover it when you enter the frontier of your deep desires.

- Ultimately, this means you forsake a careful life that depends on formulas in exchange for an intimate, conversational walk with God.

DISCUSS

❖ There's nothing quite like the feeling of overcoming a fear and discovering the thrill of freedom. Have you ever had an experience in which you embraced an adventure in spite of your fears and discovered the thrill of living freely, if only for an afternoon? What was it?

PART 6

❖ What in this DVD session struck you as the most important, the most relevant point?

Why does God create Adam? What is a man for? If you know what something is designed to do, then you know its purpose in life. A retriever loves the water; a lion loves the hunt; a hawk loves to soar. It's what they're made for. Desire reveals design, and design reveals destiny. In the case of human beings, our design is also revealed by our desires. . . . Most men think they are simply here on earth to kill time—and it's killing them. But the truth is precisely the opposite. The secret longing of your heart, whether it's to build a boat and sail it, to write a symphony and play it, to plant a field and care for it—those are the things you were made to do. That's what you're here for. Explore, build, conquer—you don't have to tell a boy to do those things for the simple reason that it *is his purpose.*[1]

❖ Why did God create you?

I opened this video with the statement "Don't ask yourself what the world needs; ask yourself what makes you come alive, and go and do that. Because what the world needs are men who have come alive."

❖ Which has guided you more in your career and life choices: what the world needs or what makes you come alive? Or have you had a different motivation? Why?

We talked about the Bible as one adventure story after another—Abraham leaving everything he'd known, Jonah being called to a place he didn't want to go, Peter walking on the water.

❖ Has Christianity felt like a great adventure to you? Why or why not?

When God gets ahold of a man, he calls him into an adventure. His invitation to every man requires adventure because he wants us to live by faith. We prefer control over risk, over faith, over following God. But when a man plays it safe, he's confessing that he doesn't trust God.

❖ Consider the statement, "When a man plays it safe he's confessing that he doesn't trust God"? Do you agree or disagree?

❖ Which of the following is your response to all the normal fears of risk, failure, and the unknown that God's adventures cause to surface in your heart?

- To shrink back, as so many of us have done before, and reject the invitation to adventure;

- to try to reach for some sort of formula that will give you a sense of control; or

- to simply venture forward with God?

❖ What adventures is God calling you to now? Are they adventures that you can't do alone—where, if God doesn't show up, you're hosed?

God calls every man out of the boat and onto the water. Many hesitate, living at the level of formulaic approach to life versus an intimate conversational relationship with God.

❖ Why do so many have this hesitancy? Do you?

PRAYER

If our adventure isn't God-given, it's just another selfish pursuit. Check in with God, and ask him to reveal to you his purposes for your life. What adventure is he calling you to embark on?

Lord, I want to love with much more abandon and stop waiting for others to love me first. I want to hurl myself into a creative work worthy of you, God. I want to charge the beaches at Normandy, follow Peter as he followed you out onto the sea. Place within me your great heart so that I may live the adventure you have for me. In Jesus' name. Amen.

The Lord had said to Abram, "Leave your country, your people and your father's household
and go to the land I will show you" . . .
So Abram left, as the LORD had told him.

—Genesis 12:1, 4

GOING DEEPER

Take the time to read through chapter 11 from *Wild at Heart* and answer these questions on your own this week.

⸻

❖ First, how did the group conversation and interaction go this week?

❖ Did you feel diminished or strong listening to the stories of other men's adventures?

❖ What did God impress you with or say to you as you were meeting with the men?

Too many men forsake their dreams because they aren't willing to risk, or they fear they aren't up to the challenge, or they've never been told that those desires deep in their heart are *good*. Recall some of the adventures you've had in the major seasons of your life.

❖ When did you *really* experience freedom and exhilaration, take a risk, and come alive . . .

- As a boy?

- As a teen/young man?

- As an adult?

PART 6

The diagram below divides men into four groups based on how much they embrace God and risk. Men in Quadrant 1 may be spiritual, but it's a safe or controlling spirituality. These are hesitant men who justify their fear by calling it caution. Or, they might be controlling men, who practice their religion as tips and techniques for controlling their world. (I might note that if a man moves up the vertical axis toward a true intimacy with God, he won't stay in Quadrant 1 for long. God will hurl him into Quadrant 4.)

The men in Quadrant 2 are also men who live "safely," but they have no spiritual disguise for it. They hide behind the newspaper or their work.

Men in Quadrant 3 may be entrepreneurs or they may be gamblers or extreme sports addicts. They are men with a great deal of so-called adventure in their lives, but it is a totally godless adventure.

Men in Quadrant 4 are guys like King David or the apostle Paul or Christopher Columbus—men who venture forth on a quest of great risk because they are walking with God.

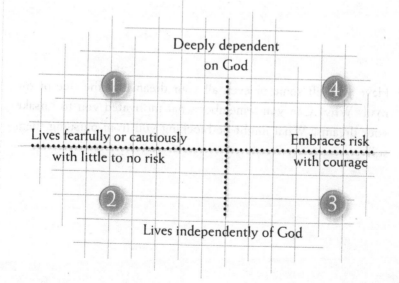

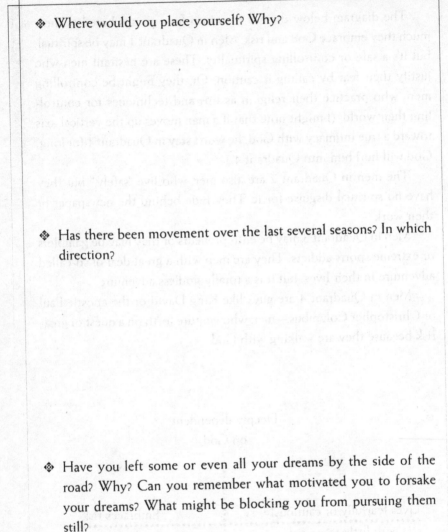

❖ Where would you place yourself? Why?

❖ Has there been movement over the last several seasons? In which direction?

❖ Have you left some or even all your dreams by the side of the road? Why? Can you remember what motivated you to forsake your dreams? What might be blocking you from pursuing them still?

❖ Start making a list of all the things you deeply desire to do with your life, great and small. And remember—don't ask yourself how. "How?" is never the right question. "How?" is a faithless question. "How?" is God's department. He is asking you, "What?" What is written on your heart? What makes you come alive? If you could do what you've always wanted to do, what would it be?

God is a person, not a doctrine. He operates not like a system— not even a theological system—but with all the originality of a truly free and alive person. "The realm of God is dangerous," Archbishop Anthony Bloom says. "You must enter into it and not just seek information about it." The only way to live in this adventure—with all its danger and unpredictability and immensely high stakes—is in an ongoing, intimate relationship with God.

❖ Do you think conversational intimacy, where God speaks to you personally, is available to you? If not, why not? What is your position based on—Scripture, or experience?

My guess is, the journey that now lies ahead of you doesn't seem real clear. Am I right? That's not a bad sign—that doesn't mean you're not "getting it." Not at all. The call of God always, *in every case*, requires deeper intimacy with God. I don't know one man to whom God has given the entire game plan for his life. Not one. You want to know something fascinating? Not even Jesus has the full game plan . . .

All God usually reveals to us is a big vision, written in our desire, and the next couple of steps. Consider that an act of mercy. If he had told you all that was going to happen in your life up to *this* point, would you have really wanted to know?[2]

PRAYER

Spend time talking with God about your adventure, the desires he's put in your heart, and the desires beneath those desires. What have you held on to and what have you abandoned? Why? Pray again, in your own words this time, the prayer on page 80.

NEXT WEEK

Next week your group will discuss the seventh DVD segment, "A Beauty to Rescue." In order to be prepared to share your thoughts with your group, read chapter 10 from *Wild at Heart* this week prior to your group meeting.

NOTES

PART

7

A BEAUTY TO RESCUE

I belong to my lover, and
his desire is for me.

—Song of Songs 7:10

The beauty of a woman arouses a man to play the man. The strength of a man, offered tenderly to his woman, allows her to be beautiful. It brings life to her and many. This is a reality that extends to every aspect of our lives. When a man withholds himself from his woman, he leaves her without the life only he can bring.

WATCH PART 7:
A BEAUTY TO RESCUE

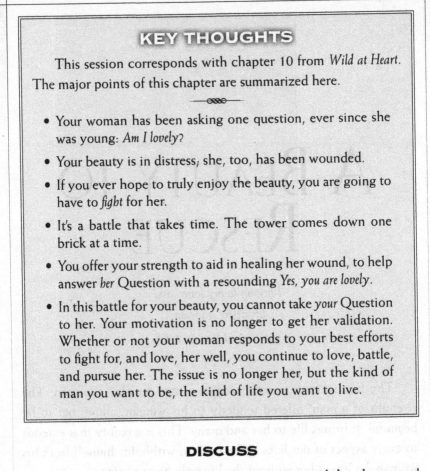

KEY THOUGHTS

This session corresponds with chapter 10 from *Wild at Heart*. The major points of this chapter are summarized here.

——⚬♦♦⚬——

- Your woman has been asking one question, ever since she was young: *Am I lovely?*

- Your beauty is in distress; she, too, has been wounded.

- If you ever hope to truly enjoy the beauty, you are going to have to *fight* for her.

- It's a battle that takes time. The tower comes down one brick at a time.

- You offer your strength to aid in healing her wound, to help answer *her* Question with a resounding *Yes, you are lovely.*

- In this battle for your beauty, you cannot take *your* Question to her. Your motivation is no longer to get her validation. Whether or not your woman responds to your best efforts to fight for, and love, her well, you continue to love, battle, and pursue her. The issue is no longer her, but the kind of man you want to be, the kind of life you want to live.

DISCUSS

Some guys were little Don Juans, running around the playground at school, kissing girls left and right. Others were more reserved, not coming into their own until high school or college.

❖ Who was your first crush? What did you like about her, and what happened between you and her?

As I prepared for the filming of this DVD session, with our wives invited, no script written, and cameras running, I pointed out the obvious, saying, "No day has been filled with more mystery than this coming adventure. To invite our wives in and give them permission to be honest and tell whatever is on their hearts, to be true about what we have done and what they desire with us . . . let's go rappel, without a rope! I feel like, whoa, this is a big cliff for me personally."

❖ What would race through your mind in our situation: your wife going on camera to record her thoughts about you as a man?

❖ How do you feel in the presence of your woman? (Thrilled, threatened, engaged, strong, like a child, alive, self-protective, loving?)

Just as every little boy is asking one Question, every little girl is, as well. The deep cry of a little girl's heart is, *Am I lovely?* Every woman needs to know that she is exquisite and exotic and *chosen*. This is core to her identity, the way she bears the image of God. She wonders, *Will you pursue me? Do you delight in me? Will you fight for me?*

❖ Do you see this core longing—to be pursued, to be delighted in, to be fought for—in your beauty's life today? How? Where?

❖ If she doesn't seem to care at all about being deeply desired and fought for, what does that tell you about what's happened to her heart?

❖ As you listened to our wives, what stood out to you? What did you learn about a woman's wound?

❖ One of Adam's greatest failings was his passivity with Eve. He simply stood by and watched her fall; he didn't step in to rescue her. How have you been silent or passive, running from the hard places of being a man with a woman?

Most men take their souls' search for validation to the woman, but she can never give him what he can only find in God. Until he's found the answer to his Question, he is preoccupied with his own quest. A man cannot fight for his beauty if he is still taking his Question to her.

❖ Are you aware of how you've taken your Question to your beauty over the years? How might you be doing it even now?

❖ In the video you saw us ask the women how we have added to their wounds, and how we have fought for them. Do you know what your woman's wound is? How have you added to it?

If I told you that you needed to do something to move toward your wife, to invite her into adventure, there are some ideas that would come to you that you would dread acting on.

❖ What step closer to your beauty feels really risky to you? Where and how do you see a need to move toward your woman?

❖ What do you need to do now to fight for her?

I want to offer two very strong words of warning, or maybe, words of *encouragement* as you plan your movement back toward your woman. First, the "tower" that has held your wife's heart—and the defenses she's added herself—it usually comes down one brick at a time. That might seem discouraging at first, but only if you want a quick fix, in which case you're not really talking about playing the man at all. If you are, it's helpful to know it takes time, and all of us falter at first. Don't get discouraged if it feels like two steps forward, one step back. That's how it goes. You don't undo decades of damage in a day.

Second, this cannot be about *your* Question. Remember, ever since the Fall, Eve has been a bottomless pit. You'll offer some wonderful words, and she'll love them . . . and they won't fill her. It will, in some ways, never be "enough." YOU CANNOT TAKE HER RESPONSE AS THE REPORT CARD ON YOU. Keep taking *your* Question to God; ask *him* how you're doing.[1]

PRAYER

If you're serious about pursuing the beauty in your life, you'll let God direct your footsteps. Go to him in prayer about your relationship with the woman in your life.

Dear God, forgive me for living a selfish, self-protecting life. Forgive me for not spending my life on behalf of my woman, and for all the wounds I've given her. Grant me the grace to undo that damage and bring that tower down. Jesus, awaken me to the real battle for her; expose the enemy and his tactics against her and against our marriage. Give me your fierce love, your jealous love, for my wife and for her freedom. And grant me courage, cunning, and selflessness as I fight for her. I ask this in your name. Amen.

I stood up and said to the nobles, the offi-
cials and the rest of the people,
"Don't be afraid of them. Remember the
Lord, who is great and awesome,
and fight for your brothers, your sons and your daughters,
your wives and your homes."
—Nehemiah 4:14

GOING DEEPER

This battle cuts to the quick of our own masculinity more than any other. To charge the beaches at Normandy and be taken out by a mortar shell isn't anywhere as personal as going in after your wife and having her shut you down—or laugh in your face. We've stayed clear of this battle for a reason. Read chapter 10 from *Wild at Heart* again and answer the questions on your own this week.

❖ What are you feeling as you think of fighting for your wife's heart, going to a whole new level in your relationship, into waters you've never sailed before?

To battle for your wife, you'll need to know not only what her childhood wounds were, but also how you've contributed to them. I confessed that when Stasi married me, she married a frightened, driven man who had an affair with his work because he wouldn't risk engaging a woman he sensed he wasn't enough for.

❖ What kind of man did your wife marry when she married you?

She's been wounded, just like you. Some wounds are obvious, like sexual abuse. Others, like neglect, are harder to see. (She may not even see it at this point.) But because of this broken world, every woman carries a wound at the core of her heart of beauty, and the wound always brings a message with it: *No. You're not beautiful, and no one will really fight for you.* As your wound did, hers probably came from her father also.

- ❖ Have you asked or has your wife ever told you about her wound and how she received it?

- ❖ If not, do you have a hunch what the message given to her by her father was? How did he speak to her heart's deepest Question?

In the battle for your woman's heart, you will need to understand her wound and how [she received it]. But this is the scariest place she will ever go with you. You can't just barge in and ask; you must *earn* the right to go there, to be trusted with this.[2]

Imagine you make the decision to pursue your woman, to fight for her heart. Then one day, in a year or two, she looks into your eyes and says, "You have given me something I never thought possible. You've fought for me so amazingly, you've given me such adventure, and I know I am beautiful because of you. Come and enjoy my beauty."

❖ What does the thought of that stir in you, or is it so far from your current reality that it simply seems unreachable?

A lover gives himself to his beauty, offering his strength to tear down the walls of her tower and speak to her heart's deepest Question in a thousand ways. *Yes, you are lovely. Yes, there is someone who will fight for you.* We offer our words and actions to express our delight in her. But this starts with *words.* I know, I know—it's common knowledge that a woman uses thousands more words each day than a man, that men don't communicate verbally, and all that. Most of it is excuses. Your woman craves words from you, longs for conversation with you. Offer it. This is not going to kill you.

❖ How many times a week do you tell your wife that you love her?

❖ How many times a week do you tell your wife that she is lovely or pretty, that she looks great, or that you like what she's wearing?

❖ And in a given week, is it common for the two of you to have a personal conversation about your life or hers, one that lasts more than five minutes?

There's no formula for this, but if you're not speaking to her heart's desire to be delighted in daily, if intimate conversations are less than weekly, you're starving her. Ante up, brother. Now let's look at your actions:

❖ How often do you offer your wife physical attention without expecting it to lead to sex?

❖ How often do you hold hands, sit on the couch, and cuddle as you watch a movie, or give her a hug or a kiss with nothing else in mind?

❖ And have you given her flowers, a card, or a gift, or taken her to dinner or on a getaway trip *for no reason whatsoever*?

❖ What is one word you will say and one action you will do this week to win the heart of your beauty?

PRAYER

End your time here praying for your beauty. In your own words, pray the prayer given for your group time on page 96.

NEXT WEEK

Next week your group will discuss the final DVD segment, "A Band of Brothers." It will be your last session together, so pray between now and your next meeting about where you would like to go from here as a group of men.

NOTES

PART

8

A BAND OF BROTHERS

All the believers were one in heart.

—Acts 4:32

This is the eighth and final session of this DVD series . . . but it's not intended to be the end. Far from it. One of the hopes of this series is to bind men together into little platoons or bands of brothers. The five of us couldn't imagine "doing life" without one another; it would be like loading a barn full of hay by yourself . . . long, hard, and lonely.

WATCH PART 8:
A BAND OF BROTHERS

KEY THOUGHTS

- Bands of Brothers are necessary and available. God is calling together little communities of men to fight for one another and for the hearts of those who have not yet been set free. That camaraderie, that intimacy, that incredible impact by a few stouthearted souls—that is available. It is the Christian life as Jesus gave it to us. It is completely normal.

- A Band of Brothers must be small. Is it possible for a hundred men who gather for an hour on a Sunday morning or Wednesday evening to really and truly know each other? It can't be done. They can't possibly be intimate allies. It can be inspiring and encouraging to celebrate with a big ol' crowd of men, but who will fight for your heart?

- A Band of Brothers must be intimate. The sort of devotion we want and need takes place within a shared life. We adventure together, help one another move, paint a room, find work. We throw great parties. We fight for each other. This is how it was meant to be. I love this description of the early church: "All the believers were one in heart" (Acts 4:32). A camaraderie was being expressed there, a bond, an esprit de corps. It means they all loved the same thing, wanted the same thing, and they were bonded together to find it, come hell or high water.

- A Band of Brothers will be messy. It is a royal mess. I will not whitewash this. It is disruptive. Going to church or a men's group with hundreds of other people to sit and hear a sermon doesn't ask much of you. It certainly will never expose you. That's why most folks prefer it. But community will. It will reveal where you have yet to become holy, right at the very moment you are so keenly aware of how they have yet to become holy. It will bring you close, and you will be seen and you will be known, and therein lies the power and therein lies the danger.

- You will have to fight for it. A true community is something you'll have to fight for. You'll have to fight both to get one, and to keep it afloat. But you fight for it as you bail out a life raft during a storm at sea. You want this thing to work. You need this thing to work. You can't ditch it and jump back on the cruise ship. This is the church; this is all you have. Without it, you'll go down. Or back to captivity. This is the reason those small house fellowships thrive in other countries: they need each other. There are no other options.

DISCUSS

❖ What have you enjoyed the most about this Band of Brothers group? Were your goals and hopes for the group (that you expressed in Part 1) met?

Over the last eight weeks, you've watched us do a bit of life together. We've rappelled, rafted together, fished, worked, laughed, and even put on a dinner for our wives. We've been pretty vulnerable about our posing, desires, wounds, and journeys.

❖ What similarities and differences have you seen between our group and yours? What would you do to increase the intimacy and fulfill-ment within your group?

To give yourself to a group like this, carving out the time to read, reflect, and meet is an enormous indicator of your heart's desire to grow as a man and a follower of Christ. Well done! It's pretty easy to stay in the passivity of Adam and do very little to care for your mas-culine heart.

❖ What has God done in your life through these eight sessions together? What new habits have you developed as a result of join-ing this group?

We hear each other's stories. We learn to walk with God together. We pray for each other's healing. We cover each other's backs. This small core fellowship is the essential ingredient for the Christian life. Jesus modeled it for us for a reason. Sure, he spoke to the masses. But he lived in a little platoon, a small fellowship of friends and allies. His followers took his example and lived this way too (see Acts 2:46; 1 Corinthians 16:19; and Colossians 4:15).

❖ Have you seen the importance of and emphasis given to small groups meeting in the life of Christ and throughout the New Testament?

Seriously, now—how often have you seen this sort of intimate community work? It is rare. Because it is hard, and it is fiercely opposed. The enemy hates this sort of thing; he knows how powerful it can be, for God and his kingdom. For our hearts. It is devastating to him. We have settled for safety in numbers—a comfortable, anonymous distance. An army that keeps meeting for briefings, but never breaks into platoons and goes to war.

❖ A Band of Brothers or any life-giving small group is difficult to pull off, and many are miserable experiences. What is appealing and what concerns you about a regular gathering of a small group of men?

❖ Do friendships with men come easily for you? Why or why not?

In talking on the DVD about the value of a Band of Brothers, I share how each of the guys "calls out of me some part that God is working on, glorifying, calling forth, and wants me to live out of. I can't be my full self without the Band of Brothers." Bart adds, "You guys have really affirmed in me that I can do what my deepest heart's desire is and what I really want to do: to be a part of a larger story."

❖ From your experience, what's missing in most men's accountability groups?

With this being the final session, we shared some final words with you:

Craig offered, "All of this is available . . . it's out there. God will provide it . . . Don't let resignation take you down."

Gary's advice was, "There is a battle and a place for every man. God has equipped every man for his place, that's written on your heart, so you have to find your heart."

Morgan's input was, "Stay in the battle . . . and you'll change the world."

Bart added, "You've got to step into the unknown . . . leaving the comfort of a small story."

And my thoughts are, in simple terms, you've got to get your heart back—everything else flows from there. Find your place in the battle. All of this will not come quickly, but it will come! Learn to fight. Let God father you in battle, adventure, and pursuing the beauty.

❖ What final words ring truest to you and your heart at this time?

❖ How are you going to hang on to what you've learned during these eight weeks?

It is not the critic who counts; not the man who points out how the strong man stumbles, or where the doer of deeds could have done them better. The credit belongs to the man in the arena, whose face is marred by dust and sweat and blood, who strives valiantly . . . who knows the great enthusiasms, the great devotions; who spends himself in a worthy cause; who at the best knows in the end the triumph of high achievement, and who at the worst, if he fails, at least fails while daring greatly, so that his place shall never be with those cold and timid souls who have never known neither victory nor defeat.

—Teddy Roosevelt

The floor of the arena is messy, and it can be confusing; it requires courage and it fosters strength . . . And, really, where else would you rather be?

❖ What are your thoughts about your need for a Band of Brothers? And continuing with this group of men?

PRAYER

Spend time in prayer exploring the next steps for this group of men. What is God laying on your heart for the future of this Band of Brothers?

———— ⚭ ————

Lord, I thank you for this season with this group of men. You've come and moved among us, speaking into our masculine hearts and inviting us into the life and freedom of your gospel as men. We ask that the work you've begun in each of us continue. We give you permission to work, to speak, to heal and restore our hearts.

Lord, guide us as men into this next season. What would you have each of us do? We surrender; we yield ourselves to you and your good intentions for our lives. Amen.

And let us consider how we may spur one another
on toward love and good deeds. Let us not give
up meeting together, as some are in the habit of
doing, but let us encourage one another.

—Hebrews 10:24–25

GOING DEEPER

❖ How was your conversation and interaction in this last session? What were you feeling as you discussed the future of this group and its continuation?

❖ Did you find yourself reluctant to share your thoughts? Did you temper them or regret saying too much?

❖ What did God impress you with or say to you as you were meeting with the men?

Let your heart ponder this: You awake to find yourself in the midst of a great and terrible war. It is, in fact, our most desperate hour. Your King and dearest Friend calls you forth. Awake, come fully alive, your good heart set free and blazing for him and for those yet to be rescued. You have a glory that is needed. You are given a quest, a mission that will take you deep into the heart of the kingdom of darkness, to break down gates of bronze and cut through bars of iron so that your people might be set free from their bleak prisons. He asks that you heal them. Of course, you will face many dangers; you will be hunted. Would you try to do this alone? . . .

Imagine you *could* have a little fellowship of the heart. Would you want it if it were available?[1]

PART 8

❖ Can you really live the Christian life alone? Have you tried? How did it go if you have?

❖ How strong is the desire on your part to lead a new group of men through this material or to continue with your current group of men in a different study?

❖ To what great battle would you love to devote your life? What do you want to change about the world or about the church or about someone's life?

- And what is the next step, the next move you need to make toward that vision?

- Into what great adventure would you love to enter? (No doubt all three of these Core Desires are going to be related somehow.) What quest would you love to take?

- And what is the next step, the next move you need to make toward that vision?

❖ Who is the woman God has called you to fight for? (Of course, some of you won't have an answer for this right now. That's okay. This can apply to women in your family, female friends, or the woman who may one day come.) What is the impact you want your life to have upon hers?

❖ And what is the next step you need to take in order to move toward her, to fight for her?

PRAYER

Worship God, thanking him for the things he's spoken to you during this study. Ask him to imprint these things on your heart, so that you will not forget the lessons he's given you.

A NOTE FROM THE AUTHOR

Where do you go from here? Let me offer some counsel for your journey now. Read the book again. There is no way you have gotten all that God has for you in one reading—the scope of the journey is too great, and our needs for validation, direction, healing, and initiation too great to perceive all at once.

Another great resource is *Fathered by God*. The path to manhood is a journey of discovery and experience, trial, and adventure. Get a few guys together and go through the book as a Band of Brothers. There is a Participant's Guide available. These materials come alongside those men who long to have a guide to lead them through this rite of passage, this masculine initiation. Filled with personal stories, illustrations from popular movies and books, and probing questions, this material will set you on a heart-searching expedition to become the man God sees in you.

Then what? Come to Ransomedheart.com and you will find there many tools and maps for your initiation—like our audio series, *The Hope of Prayer,* and *The Utter Relief of Holiness*. We offer camps and retreats for men, and podcasts. Come, and continue the journey!

Of course, you know now that my counsel will always first and foremost be, "Ask God." He knows what you need next. Ask him what he has for you—what friends, what adventures, what battles, what help he has in store. Be intentional. "Those who are led by the Spirit of God are sons of God" (Romans 8:14).

APPENDIX: A DAILY PRAYER FOR FREEDOM

My dear Lord Jesus, I come to you now to be restored in you—to renew my place in you, my allegiance to you, and to receive from you all the grace and mercy I so desperately need this day. I honor you as my sovereign Lord, and I surrender every aspect of my life totally and completely to you. I give you my body as a living sacrifice; I give you my heart, soul, mind, and strength; and I give you my spirit as well. I cover myself with your blood—my spirit, my soul, and my body. And I ask your Holy Spirit to restore my union with you, seal me in you, and guide me in this time of prayer. In all that I now pray, I include [my wife, and/or my children, by name]. Acting as [her or their] head, I bring them under my authority and covering, and I come under your authority and covering. Holy Spirit, apply to them all that I now pray on their behalf.

Dear God, holy and victorious Trinity, you alone are worthy of all my worship, my heart's devotion, all my praise and all my trust and all the glory of my life. I worship you, bow to you, and give myself over to you in my heart's search for life. You alone are Life, and you have become my life. I renounce all other gods, all idols, and I give you the place in my heart and in my life that you truly deserve. I confess here and now that it is all about you, God, and not about me. You are the Hero of this story, and I belong to you. Forgive me, God, for my every sin. Search me and know me, and reveal to me any aspect of my life that is not pleasing to you. Expose any agreements I have made, and grant me the grace of a deep and true repentance.

Heavenly Father, thank you for loving me and choosing me before you made the world. You are my true Father—my Creator, my Redeemer, my Sustainer, and the true end of all things, including my life. I love you; I trust you; I worship you. Thank you for proving your love for me by sending your only Son, Jesus, to be my substitute and representative. I receive him and all his life and all his work, which you ordained for me. Thank you for including me in Christ, for forgiving me my sins, for granting me his righteousness, for making me complete in him. Thank you for making me alive with Christ, raising me with him, seating me with him at your right hand, granting me his authority, and anointing me with your Holy Spirit. I receive it all with thanks and give it total claim to my life.

Jesus, thank you for coming for me, for ransoming me with your own life. I honor you as my Lord; I love you, worship you, trust you. I sincerely receive you as my redemption, and I receive all the work and triumph of your crucifixion, whereby I am cleansed from all my sin through your shed blood; my old nature is removed, my heart is circumcised unto God, and every claim being made against me is disarmed. I take my place in your cross and death, whereby I have died with you to sin and to my flesh, to the world, and to the evil one. I am crucified with Christ, and I have crucified my flesh with all its passions and desires. I take up my cross and crucify my flesh with all its pride, unbelief, and idolatry. I put off the old man. I now bring the cross of Christ between me and all people, all spirits, all things.

Holy Spirit, apply to me [my wife and/or children] the fullness of the work of the crucifixion of Jesus Christ for me. I receive it with thanks and give it total claim to my life.

Jesus, I also sincerely receive you as my new life, my holiness and sanctification, and I receive all the work and triumph of your resurrection, whereby I have been raised with you to a new life, to walk in newness of life, dead to sin and alive to God. I am crucified with Christ, and it is no longer I who live but Christ who lives in me. I now take my place in your resurrection, whereby I have been made alive with you. I reign in life through you. I now put on the new man in all holiness and humility, in all righteousness and purity and truth. Christ is now my life, the one who strengthens me. Holy Spirit, apply to me [my wife and/or my children] the fullness of the resurrection of Jesus Christ for me. I receive it with thanks and give it total claim to my life.

Jesus, I also sincerely receive you as my authority and rule, my everlasting victory over Satan and his kingdom, and I receive all the work and triumph of your ascension, whereby Satan has been judged and cast down, and his rulers and authorities disarmed. All authority in heaven and on earth is given to you, Jesus, and I have been given fullness in you, the Head over all. I take my place in your ascension, whereby I have been raised with you to the right hand of the Father and established with you in all authority.

I bring your authority and your kingdom rule over my life, my family, my household, and my domain.

And now I bring the fullness of your work—your cross, resurrection, and ascension—against Satan, against his kingdom, and against all his emissaries and all their work warring against me and my domain. Greater is he who is in me than he who is in the world. Christ has given me authority to overcome all the power of the evil one, and I claim that authority now over and against every enemy, and I banish them in the name of Jesus Christ. Holy Spirit, apply to me [my wife and/or my children] the fullness of the work of the ascension of Jesus Christ for me. I receive it with thanks and give it total claim to my life.

Holy Spirit, I sincerely receive you as my Counselor, my Comforter, my Strength, and my Guide. Thank you for sealing me in Christ. I honor you as my Lord, and I ask you to lead me into all truth, to anoint me for all of my life and walk and calling, and to lead me deeper into Jesus today. I fully open my life to you in every dimension and aspect—my body, my soul, and my spirit—choosing to be filled with you and to walk in step with you in all things. Apply to me, blessed Holy Spirit, all of the work and all of the gifts in pentecost. Fill me afresh, blessed Holy Spirit. I receive you with thanks and give you total claim to my life [and my wife and/or children].

Heavenly Father, thank you for granting to me every spiritual blessing in the heavenlies in Christ Jesus. I receive those blessings into my life today, and I ask the Holy Spirit to bring all those blessings into my life this day. Thank you for the blood of Jesus. Wash me once more with his blood from every sin and stain and evil device. I put on your armor—the belt of truth, the breastplate of righteousness, the shoes of the readiness of the gospel of peace, and the helmet of salvation. I take up the shield of faith and the sword of the Spirit, the Word of God, and I wield these weapons against the evil one in the power of God. I choose to pray at all times in the Spirit, and to be strong in you, Lord, and in your might.

Father, thank you for your angels. I summon them in the authority of Jesus Christ and release them to war for me and my household. May they guard me at all times this day.

Thank you for those who pray for me; I confess I need their prayers, and I ask you to send forth your Spirit and rouse them, unite them, raising up the full canopy of prayer and intercession for me. I call forth the kingdom of the Lord Jesus Christ this day throughout my home, my family, my life, and my domain. I pray all of this in the name of Jesus Christ, with all glory and honor and thanks to him.

NOTES

Introduction

1. John Eldredge, *Wild at Heart* (Nashville: Thomas Nelson, 2001), 4, 5, 6.

Part 1

1. Eldredge, *Wild at Heart* (Nashville: Thomas Nelson, 2001), 8.
2. Ibid., 26.
3. Ibid., 5.

Part 2

1. John Eldredge, *Wild at Heart Field Manual* (Nashville: Thomas Nelson, 2002), 56.
2. Ibid.

Part 3

1. Eldredge, *Wild at Heart Field Manual*, 92.
2. Ibid., 94, 96, 92.

Part 4

1. Eldredge, *Wild at Heart*, 105.
2. Ibid., 88.
3. 1 Corinthians 6:17.

Part 5

1. Eldredge, *Wild at Heart*, 141–42.

Part 6

1. Eldredge, *Wild at Heart*, 48–49.
2. Eldredge, *Wild at Heart Field Manual*, 268.

Part 7

1. Eldredge, *Wild at Heart Field Manual*, 239.
2. Ibid., 231.

Part 8

1. John Eldredge, *Waking the Dead* (Nashville: Thomas Nelson, 2003), 186–88.

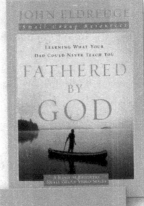
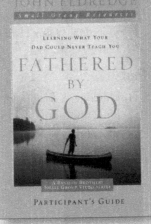

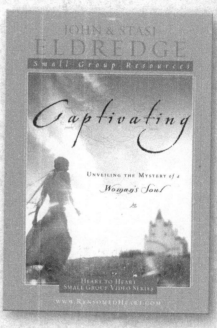